Wine FOR DUMMIES®

MINI EDITION

by Ed McCarthy and
Mary Ewing-Mulligan

WILEY

Wiley Publishing, Inc.

Y0-DAC-421

Wine For Dummies,®️ Mini Edition

Published by
Wiley Publishing, Inc.
111 River St.
Hoboken, NJ 07030-5774
www.wiley.com

For general information on our other products and services, please contact our Customer Care Department within the U.S. at 877-762-2974, outside the U.S. at 317-572-3993, or fax 317-572-4002.

For technical support, please visit www.wiley.com/techsupport.

Wiley also publishes its books in a variety of electronic formats and by print-on-demand. Some content that appears in standard print versions of this book may not be available in other formats. For more information about Wiley products, visit us at www.wiley.com.

ISBN: 978-1-118-06163-3

Manufactured in the United States of America

10 9 8 7 6 5 4 3 2 1

Table of Contents

Introduction *1*

Chapter 1: Wine 101 .... *3*

How Wine Happens...3
    What could be more natural? 4
    Modern wrinkles in winemaking...........................5
    The main ingredient 5
    Local flavor 6
What Color Is Your Appetite?.......................................6
    (Not exactly) white wine 6
    Is white always right?..7
    Red, red wine 8
    A rose is a rose, but a rosé is "white" 10
    Which type when? 10

Chapter 2: These Taste Buds Are for You... 13

The Special Technique for Tasting Wine..................14
    Savoring wine's good looks.................................14
    The nose knows 15
    The mouth action 17
Parlez-Vous Winespeak?..19
    The sequential palate..19
    The flavor dimension 21
The Quality Issue 22
    What's a good wine? 23
    What's a bad wine?..26

Chapter 3: Pinot Envy and Other Secrets about Grape Varieties 29

Why Grapes Matter 30

    Of genus and species 30

    A variety of varieties 30

    How grapes vary 31

A Primer on White Grape Varieties 32

    Chardonnay..33

    Riesling 34

    Sauvignon Blanc 35

    Pinot Gris/Pinot Grigio...............................36

A Primer on Red Grape Varieties 37

    Cabernet Sauvignon 37

    Merlot...38

    Pinot Noir 38

    Syrah/Shiraz 39

    Zinfandel 39

    Nebbiolo 40

    Sangiovese 40

    Tempranillo..41

Chapter 4: The Insider's Track to Serving and Using Wine 43

Getting the Cork Out...44

    The corkscrew not to use............................45

    The corkscrew to buy...................................45

    Other corkscrews worth owning...............47

    A special case: Opening Champagne and sparkling wine................................51

Not Too Warm, Not Too Cold.................................53

Introduction

● ●

*W*e love wine. We love the way it tastes, we love the fascinating variety of wines in the world, and we love the way wine brings people together at the dinner table. We believe that you and everyone else should be able to enjoy wine — regardless of your experience or your budget.

But we're the first to admit that wine people don't make it easy for regular people to enjoy wine. All the complication surrounding wine will never go away, because wine is a very rich and complex field. But you don't have to let the complication stand in your way. With the right attitude and a little understanding of what wine is, you can begin to buy and enjoy wine. And if, like us, you decide that wine is fascinating, you can find out more and turn it into a wonderful hobby.

Icons Used in This Book

We use the following icons in this book:

Advice or information that will make you a wiser wine drinker or buyer is marked by this bull's-eye so that you won't miss it.

There's very little you can do in the course of moderate wine consumption that can land you in jail — but you could spoil an expensive bottle and sink into a deep depression over your loss. This symbol warns you about common pitfalls.

Some wine issues are so fundamental that they bear repeating. Just so you don't think that we repeat ourselves without realizing it, we mark the repetitions with this symbol.

 Wine snobs practice all sorts of affectations designed to make other wine drinkers feel inferior. But you won't be intimidated by their snobbery if you see it for what it is. (And you can learn how to impersonate a wine snob!)

 This odd little guy is a bit like the 2-year-old who constantly insists on knowing "Why, Mommy, why?" But he knows that you may not have the same level of curiosity that he has. Where you see him, feel free to skip over the technical information that follows.

Where to Go from Here

You've got your minibook copy of *Wine For Dummies*. Now what? This minibook is a reference, so if you need information on how to open a wine bottle, head to Chapter 4. Or if you're interested in finding out about different reds or whites, head to Chapter 3. Or heck, start with Chapter 1 and read the chapters in order. If you want even more advice on wine, from navigating a wine shop to buying and collecting wine, check out the full-size version of *Wine For Dummies,* 4th Edition — simply head to your local book seller or go to www.dummies.com!

Chapter 1

Wine 101

● ●

In This Chapter

▶ Looking at what wine is

▶ Defining million-dollar words like *fermentation* and *sulfites*

▶ Identifying what red wine has that white wine doesn't

▶ Knowing why color matters

● ●

*W*e know plenty of people who enjoy drinking wine but don't know much about it. (Been there, done that ourselves.) Knowing a lot of information about wine definitely isn't a prerequisite to enjoying it. But familiarity with certain aspects of wine can make choosing wines a lot easier, enhance your enjoyment of wine, and increase your comfort level. You can learn as much or as little as you like. The journey begins here.

How Wine Happens

Wine is, essentially, nothing but liquid, fermented fruit. The recipe for turning fruit into wine goes something like this:

4

1. **Pick a large quantity of ripe grapes from grapevines.**

   You could substitute raspberries or any other fruit, but 99.9 percent of all the wine in the world is made from grapes, because they make the best wines.

2. **Put the grapes into a clean container that doesn't leak.**

3. **Crush the grapes somehow to release their juice.**

   Once upon a time, feet performed this step.

4. **Wait.**

In its most basic form, winemaking is that simple. After the grapes are crushed, *yeasts* (tiny one-celled organisms that exist naturally in the vineyard and, therefore, on the grapes) come into contact with the sugar in the grapes' juice and gradually convert that sugar into alcohol. Yeasts also produce carbon dioxide, which evaporates into the air. When the yeasts are done working, your grape juice is wine. The sugar that was in the juice is no longer there — alcohol is present instead. (The riper and sweeter the grapes, the more alcohol the wine will have.) This process is called *fermentation*.

What could be more natural?

Fermentation is a totally natural process that doesn't require man's participation at all, except to put the grapes into a container and release the juice from the grapes. Fermentation occurs in fresh apple cider left too long in your refrigerator, without any help from you. In fact, milk, which contains a different sort of sugar than grapes do, develops a small amount of alcohol if left on the kitchen table all day long.

Speaking of milk, Louis Pasteur is the man credited with discovering fermentation in the 19th century. That's discovering, not inventing. Some of those apples in the Garden of Eden probably fermented long before Pasteur came along. (Well, we don't think it could have been much of an Eden without wine!)

Modern wrinkles in winemaking

Now if every winemaker actually made wine in as crude a manner as we just described, we'd be drinking some pretty rough stuff that would hardly inspire us to write a wine book. But today's winemakers have a bag of tricks as big as a sumo wrestler's appetite. That's one reason why no two wines ever taste exactly the same.

The men and women who make wine can control the type of container they use for the fermentation process (stainless steel and oak are the two main materials), as well as the size of the container and the temperature of the juice during fermentation — and every one of these choices can make a big difference in the taste of the wine. After fermentation, they can choose how long to let the wine *mature* (a stage when the wine sort of gets its act together) and in what kind of container. Fermentation can last three days or three months, and the wine can then mature for a couple of weeks or a couple of years or anything in between. If you have trouble making decisions, don't ever become a winemaker.

The main ingredient

Obviously, one of the biggest factors in making one wine different from the next is the nature of the raw material, the grape juice. Besides the fact that riper, sweeter grapes make a more alcoholic wine, different *varieties* of grapes

(Chardonnay, Cabernet Sauvignon, or Merlot, for example) make different wines. Grapes are the main ingredient in wine, and everything the winemaker does, he does to the particular grape juice he has. Chapter 3 covers specific grapes and the kinds of wine they make.

Local flavor

Grapes, the raw material of wine, don't grow in a void. Where they grow — the soil and climate of each wine region, as well as the traditions and goals of the people who grow the grapes and make the wine — affects the nature of the ripe grapes, and the taste of the wine made from those grapes. That's why so much of the information there is to learn about wine revolves around the countries and the regions where wine is made.

What Color Is Your Appetite?

Your inner child will be happy to know that when it comes to wine, it's okay to like some colors more than others. You can't get away with saying "I don't like green food!" much beyond your sixth birthday, but you can express a general preference for white, red, or pink wine for all your adult years.

(Not exactly) white wine

Whoever coined the term *white wine* must have been colorblind. All you have to do is look at it to see that it's not white, it's yellow. But we've all gotten used to the expression by now, and so *white wine* it is.

White wine is wine without any red color (or pink color, which is in the red family). This means that *White Zinfandel,* a popular pink wine, isn't white wine. But yellow wines, golden wines, and wines that are as pale as water are all white wines.

Wine becomes white wine in one of two ways. First, white wine can be made from white grapes — which, by the way, aren't white. (Did you see that one coming?) *White* grapes are greenish, greenish yellow, golden yellow, or sometimes even pinkish yellow. Basically, white grapes include all the grape types that are not dark red or dark bluish. If you make a wine from white grapes, it's a white wine.

The second way a wine can become white is a little more complicated. The process involves using red grapes — but only the *juice* of red grapes, not the grape skins. The juice of most red grapes has no red pigmentation — only the skins do — so a wine made with only the juice of red grapes can be a white wine. In practice, though, very few white wines come from red grapes.

 In case you're wondering, the skins are removed from the grapes either by *pressing* large quantities of grapes so that the juice flows out and the skins stay behind — sort of like squeezing the pulp out of grapes, the way kids do in the cafeteria — or by *crushing* the grapes in a machine that has rollers to break the skins so that the juice can drain away.

Is white always right?

You can drink white wine anytime you like — which for most people means as a drink without food or with lighter foods.

White wines are often considered *apéritif* wines, meaning wines consumed before dinner, in place of cocktails, or at parties. (If you ask the officials who busy themselves defining such things, an apéritif wine is a wine that has flavors added to it, as vermouth does. But unless you're in the business of writing wine labels for a living, don't worry about that. In common parlance, an apéritif wine is just what we said.)

A lot of people like to drink white wines when the weather is hot because they're more refreshing than red wines, and they're usually drunk chilled (the wines, not the people).

 We serve white wines cool, but not ice cold. Sometimes restaurants serve white wines too cold, and we actually have to wait a while for the wine to warm up before we drink it. If you like your wine cold, fine; but try drinking your favorite white wine a little less cold sometime, and we bet you'll discover it has more flavor that way. In Chapter 4, we recommend specific serving temperatures for various types of wine.

For really detailed information about white wine and food (and white wine itself, for that matter), refer to our book *White Wine For Dummies* (Wiley).

Red, red wine

In this case, the name is correct. Red wines really are red. They can be purple red, ruby red, or garnet, but they're red.

Red wines are made from grapes that are red or bluish in color. So guess what wine people call these grapes? Black grapes! We suppose that's because black is the opposite of white.

 The most obvious difference between red wine and white wine is color. The red color occurs when the colorless juice of red grapes stays in contact with the dark grape skins during fermentation and absorbs the skins' color. Along with color, the grape skins give the wine *tannin,* a substance that's an important part of the way a red wine tastes. (See Chapter 2 for more about tannin.) The presence of tannin in red wines is actually the most important taste difference between red wines and white wines.

Red wines vary quite a lot in style. This is partly because winemakers have so many ways of adjusting their red-winemaking to achieve the kind of wine they want. For example, if winemakers leave the juice in contact with the skins for a long time, the wine becomes more *tannic* (firmer in the mouth, like strong tea; tannic wines can make you pucker). If winemakers drain the juice off the skins sooner, the wine is softer and less tannic.

Red wine tends to be consumed more often as part of a meal than as a drink on its own.

Thanks to the wide range of red wine styles, you can find red wines to go with just about every type of food and every occasion when you want to drink wine (except the times when you want to drink a wine with bubbles, because most bubbly wines are white or pink). For tips on matching red wine with food, check out our book *Red Wine For Dummies* (Wiley).

One sure way to spoil the fun in drinking most red wines is to drink them too cold. Those tannins can taste really bitter when the wine is cold — just as in a cold glass of very strong tea. On the other hand, many restaurants serve red wines too warm. (Where do they store them? Next to the boiler?) If the bottle feels cool to your hand, that's a good temperature. For more about serving wine at the right temperature, see Chapter 4.

A rose is a rose, but a rosé is "white"

Rosé wines are pink wines. Rosé wines are made from red grapes, but they don't end up red because the grape juice stays in contact with the red skins for a very short time — only a few hours, compared to days or weeks for red wines. Because this *skin contact* (the period when the juice and the skins intermingle) is brief, rosé wines absorb very little tannin from the skins. Therefore, you can chill rosé wines and drink them as you would white wines.

Of course, not all rosé wines are called rosés. (That would be too simple.) Many rosé wines today are called *blush* wines — a term invented by wine marketers to avoid the word *rosé,* because back in the 1980s, pink wines weren't very popular. Lest someone figures out that *blush* is a synonym for *rosé,* the labels call these wines *white.* But even a child can see that White Zinfandel is really pink.

The blush wines that call themselves *white* are fairly sweet. Wines labeled *rosé* can be sweetish, too, but some wonderful rosés from Europe (and a few from America, too) are *dry* (not sweet). Some hard-core wine lovers hardly ever drink rosé wine, but many wine drinkers are discovering what a pleasure a good rosé wine can be, especially in warm weather.

Which type when?

Your choice of a white wine, red wine, or rosé wine will vary with the season, the occasion, and the type of food that you're eating (not to mention your personal taste!). Choosing a color usually is the starting point for selecting a specific wine in a wine shop or in a restaurant. Most stores and most restaurant wine lists arrange wines by color before making other distinctions, such as grape varieties, wine regions, or taste categories.

Although certain foods can straddle the line between white wine and red wine compatibility — grilled salmon, for example, can be delicious with a rich white wine or a fruity red — your preference for red, white, or pink wine will often be your first consideration in pairing wine with food, too.

Pairing food and wine is one of the most fun aspects of wine, because the possible combinations are almost limitless. Best of all, your personal taste rules!

Chapter 2

These Taste Buds Are for You

In This Chapter
▶ Knowing how to slurp and gurgle
▶ Identifying aromas you can smell in wine
▶ Being aware of aromas you shouldn't smell in wine
▶ Recognizing the effect of acidity, tannin, and alcohol
▶ Focusing on five mysterious concepts of wine quality

*W*e know they're out there — the cynics who are saying, right about now, "Hey, I already know how to taste. All that wine-tasting humbug is just another way of making wine complicated." And you know, in a way, those cynics are right. Anyone who can taste coffee or a hamburger can taste wine. All you need are a nose, taste buds, and a brain.

You also have all that it takes to speak Mandarin. Having the ability to do something is different from knowing how to do it and applying that know-how in everyday life, however. In this chapter, we tell you how to taste.

The Special Technique for Tasting Wine

You drink beverages every day, tasting them as they pass through your mouth. In the case of wine, however, drinking and tasting are not synonymous. Wine is much more complex than other beverages: There's more going on in a mouthful of wine. For example, most wines have a lot of different (and subtle) flavors, all at the same time, and they give you multiple sensations when they're in your mouth, such as softness and sharpness together.

If you just drink wine, gulping it down the way you do soda, you miss a lot of what you paid for. But if you *taste* wine, you can discover its nuances. In fact, the more slowly and attentively you taste wine, the more interesting it tastes.

 And with that, we have the two fundamental rules of wine tasting: Slow down, and pay attention.

The process of tasting a wine — of systematically experiencing all the wine's attributes — has three steps. The first two steps don't actually involve your mouth at all. First you look at the wine, and then you smell it.

Savoring wine's good looks

We enjoy looking at the wine in our glass, noticing how brilliant it is and the way it reflects the light, trying to decide precisely which shade of red it is and whether it will stain the tablecloth permanently if we tilt the glass too far.

To observe a wine's appearance, tilt a (half-full) glass away from you and look at the color of the wine against a white background, such as the tablecloth or a piece of paper (a colored background distorts the color of the wine). Notice how dark or how pale the wine is, what color it is, and whether the color fades from the center of the wine out toward the edge, where it touches the glass. Also notice whether the wine is cloudy, clear, or brilliant. Eventually, you'll begin to notice patterns, such as deeper color in younger red wines.

The nose knows

Now we get to the really fun part of tasting wine: swirling and sniffing. This is when you can let your imagination run wild, and no one will ever dare to contradict you. If you say that a wine smells like wild strawberries to you, how can anyone prove that it doesn't?

Before you sniff, keep your glass on the table and rotate it three or four times so that the wine swirls around inside the glass and mixes with air. Then quickly bring the glass to your nose. Stick your nose into the airspace of the glass, and smell the wine. Free-associate. Is the aroma fruity, woodsy, fresh, cooked, intense, light? Your nose tires quickly, but it recovers quickly, too. Wait just a moment and try again. Listen to your friends' comments and try to find the same things they find in the smell.

The point behind this whole ritual of swirling and sniffing is that what you smell should be pleasurable to you, maybe even fascinating, and that you should have fun in the process.

Hang around wine geeks for a while, and you'll start to hear words like *petrol, manure, sweaty saddle, burnt match,* and *asparagus* used to describe the aromas of some wines. "Yuck!" you say? Of course you do! Fortunately, the wines that exhibit such smells are not the wines you'll be drinking for the most part — at least not unless you really catch the wine bug. And when you do catch the wine bug, you may discover that those aromas, in the right wine, can really be a kick. Even if you don't learn to enjoy those smells (some of us do, honest!), you'll appreciate them as typical characteristics of certain regions or grapes.

Then there are the bad smells that nobody will try to defend. It doesn't happen often, but it does happen, because wine is a natural, agricultural product with a will of its own. Often when a wine is seriously flawed, it shows immediately in the nose of the wine. Wine judges have a term for such wines. They call them DNPIM — Do Not Put In Mouth. Not that you'll get ill, but why subject your taste buds to the same abuse that your nose just took? Sometimes it's a bad cork that's to blame, and sometimes it's some other sort of problem in the winemaking or even the storage of the wine. Just rack it up to experience and open a different bottle.

While you're choosing the next bottle, make up your own acronyms: SOTYWE (Serve Only To Your Worst Enemies) for example, or ETMYG (Enough To Make You Gag), or our own favorite, SLADDR (Smells Like A Dirty Dish Rag).

When it comes to smelling wine, many people are concerned that they aren't able to detect as many aromas as they think they should. Smelling wine is really just a matter of practice and attention. If you start to pay more attention to smells in your normal activities, you'll get better at smelling wine.

The mouth action

After you've looked at the wine and smelled it, you're finally allowed to taste it. This is when grown men and women sit around and make strange faces, gurgling the wine and sloshing it around in their mouths with looks of intense concentration in their eyes. You can make an enemy for life if you distract a wine taster just at the moment when he is focusing all his energy on the last few drops of a special wine.

Here's how the procedure goes: Take a medium-size sip of wine. Hold it in your mouth, purse your lips, and draw in some air across your tongue, over the wine. (Be utterly careful not to choke or dribble, or everyone will strongly suspect that you're not a wine expert.) Then swish the wine around in your mouth as if you're chewing it. Then swallow it. The whole process should take several seconds, depending on how much you're concentrating on the wine.

Taste buds on the tongue can register various sensations, which are known as the basic tastes. These include sweetness, sourness, saltiness, bitterness, and *umami* (a savory characteristic). Of these tastes, sweetness, sourness, and bitterness are those most commonly found in wine. By moving the wine around in your mouth, you give it a chance to hit all your taste buds so that you don't miss anything in the wine (even if sourness and bitterness sound like things you wouldn't mind missing).

As you swish the wine around in your mouth, you're also buying time. Your brain needs a few seconds to figure out what the tongue is tasting and make some sense of it. Any sweetness in the wine registers in your brain first because many of the taste buds on the front of your tongue — where the wine hits first — capture the sensation of sweetness; *acidity* (which, by the way, is what normal people call sourness) and bitterness register subsequently. While your brain is working out the relative impressions of sweetness, acidity, and bitterness, you can be thinking about how the wine feels in your mouth — whether it's heavy, light, smooth, rough, and so on.

Until you cut your nose in on the action, those three sensations of sweetness, acidity, and bitterness, and a general impression of weight and texture, are all you can taste in the wine. Where have all the wild strawberries gone?

They're still there in the wine, right next to the chocolate and plums. But to be perfectly correct about it, these flavors are actually *aromas* that you taste, not through tongue contact, but by inhaling them up an interior nasal passage in the back of your mouth. When you draw in air across the wine in your mouth, you're vaporizing the aromas just as you did when you swirled the wine in your glass. There's a method to this madness.

After you go through all this rigmarole, it's time to reach a conclusion: Do you like what you tasted? The possible answers are yes, no, an indifferent shrug of the shoulders, or "I'm not sure, let me take another taste," which means that you have serious wine-nerd potential.

Parlez-Vous Winespeak?

Now we have to confess that there is one step between knowing how to taste wine and always drinking wine that you like — and it's a doozy. That step is putting taste into words.

We wouldn't have to bother with this detail if only we could always choose our wines the way that customers choose cheese in a gourmet shop. ("Can I try that one? No, I don't like it; let me taste the one next to it. Good. I'll take half a pound.")

"Like/don't like" is a no-brainer once you have the wine in your mouth. But most of the time, you have to buy the stuff without tasting it first. So unless you want to drink the same wine for the rest of your life, you're going to have to decide what it is that you like or don't like in a wine and communicate that to another person who can steer you toward a wine you'll like.

There are two hurdles here: finding the words to describe what you like or don't like, and then getting the other person to understand what you mean. Naturally, it helps if we all speak the same language.

The sequential palate

The tastes of a wine reveal themselves sequentially as the tongue detects them, and they register in your brain. We recommend that you follow this natural sequence when you try putting words to what you're tasting:

- ✔ **Sweetness:** As soon as you put the wine into your mouth, you can usually notice sweetness or the lack of it. In winespeak, *dry* is the opposite of sweet. Classify the wine you're tasting as either *dry, off-dry* (in other words, somewhat sweet), or *sweet.*

- ✔ **Acidity:** All wine contains acid (mainly *tartaric acid,* which exists in grapes), but some wines are more acidic than others. Acidity is more of a taste factor in white wines than in reds. For white wines, acidity is the backbone of the wine's taste (it gives the wine firmness in your mouth). White wines with a high amount of acidity feel *crisp,* and those without enough acidity feel *flabby.*

  You can also sense the consequences of acidity (or the lack of it) in the overall style of the wine — whether it's a tart little number or a soft and generous sort, for example. Classify the wine you're tasting as *crisp, soft,* or "couch potato."

- ✔ **Tannin:** Tannin is a substance that exists naturally in the skins, seeds (or *pips*), and stems of grapes. Because red wines are fermented with their grape skins and pips, and because red grape varieties are generally higher in tannin than white varieties, tannin levels are far higher in red wines than in white wines. Oak barrels can also contribute tannin to wines, both reds and whites. Have you ever taken a sip of a red wine and rapidly experienced a drying-out feeling in your mouth, as if something had blotted-up all your saliva? That's tannin.

To generalize a bit, tannin is to a red wine what acidity is to a white: a backbone. Tannins alone can taste bitter, but some tannins in wine are less bitter than others. Also, other elements of the wine, such as sweetness, can mask the perception of bitterness. You sense tannin — as bitterness, or as firmness or richness of texture — mainly in the rear of your mouth and, if the amount of tannin in a wine is high, on the inside of your cheeks and on your gums. Depending on the amount and nature of its tannin, you can describe a red wine as *astringent, firm,* or *soft.*

✔ **Body:** A wine's body is an impression you get from the whole of the wine — not a basic taste that registers on your tongue. It's the impression of the weight and size of the wine in your mouth, which is usually attributable principally to a wine's alcohol. We say "impression" because, obviously, 1 ounce of any wine will occupy exactly the same space in your mouth and weigh the same as 1 ounce of any other wine. But some wines *seem* fuller, bigger, or heavier in the mouth than others. Think about the wine's fullness and weight as you taste it. Imagine that your tongue is a tiny scale and judge how much the wine is weighing it down. Classify the wine as *light-bodied, medium-bodied,* or *full-bodied.*

The flavor dimension

Wines have flavors (er, we mean *mouth aromas*), but wines don't come in a specific flavor. Though you may enjoy the suggestion of chocolate in a red wine that you're tasting, you wouldn't want to go to a wine store and ask for a chocolatey wine.

Instead, you should refer to *families of flavors* in wine. You have your *fruity wines* (the ones that make you think of all sorts of fruit when you smell them or taste them), your *earthy wines* (these make you think of minerals and rocks, walks in the forest, turning the earth in your garden, dry leaves, and so on), your *spicy wines* (cinnamon, cloves, black pepper, or Indian spices, for example), your *herbal wines* (mint, grass, hay, rosemary, and so on). . . . There are so many flavors in wine that we could go on and on, but you get the picture.

If you like a wine and want to try another wine that's similar but different (and it will always be different, we guarantee you), one method is to decide what families of flavors in the wine you like and mention that to the person selling you your next bottle.

Another aspect of flavor that's important to consider is a wine's *flavor intensity* — how much flavor the wine has, regardless of what those flavors are. Some wines are as flavorful as a Big Mac, while others have flavors as subtle as fillet of sole. Flavor intensity is a major factor in pairing wine with food, and it also helps determine how much you like a wine.

The Quality Issue

Did you notice, by any chance, that nowhere among the terms we use to describe wines are the words *great, very good,* or *good?* Instead of worrying about crisp wines, earthy wines, and medium-bodied wines, wouldn't it just be easier to walk into a wine shop and say, "Give me a very good wine for dinner tonight"? Isn't *quality* the ultimate issue — or at least, quality within your price range, also known as *value?*

Quality wines come in all colors, degrees of sweetness and dryness, and flavor profiles. Just because a wine is high quality doesn't mean that you'll actually enjoy it, any more than two thumbs up means that you'll love a particular movie. Personal taste is simply more relevant than quality in choosing a wine.

Nevertheless, degrees of quality do exist among wines. But a wine's quality is not absolute: How great a wine is or isn't depends on who's doing the judging.

The instruments that measure the quality of a wine are a human being's nose, mouth, and brain, and because we're all different, we all have different opinions on how good a wine is. The combined opinion of a group of trained, experienced palates (also known as *wine experts*) is usually considered a definitive judgment of a wine's quality.

What's a good wine?

A good wine is, above all, a wine that you like enough to drink — because the whole purpose of a wine is to give pleasure to those who drink it. After that, how good a wine is depends on how it measures up to a set of (more or less) agreed-upon standards of performance established by experienced, trained experts. These standards involve the following mysterious concepts, none of which is objectively measurable:

✔ **Balance:** Three words we talk about in the "Parlez-Vous Winespeak?" section earlier in this chapter — sweetness, acidity, and tannin — represent three of the major *components* (parts) of wine. The fourth is alcohol. Besides being one of the reasons we usually want to drink a glass of wine in the first place, alcohol is an important element of wine quality.

Balance is the relationship of these four components to one another. A wine is balanced when nothing sticks out as you taste it, like harsh tannin or too much sweetness. Most wines are balanced to most people. But if you have any pet peeves about food — if you really hate anything tart, for example, or if you never eat sweets — you may perceive some wines to be unbalanced. If you perceive them to be unbalanced, then they're unbalanced for you. (Professional tasters know their own idiosyncrasies and adjust for them when they judge wine.)

✔ **Length:** When we call wines *long* or *short,* we're not referring to the size of the bottle or how quickly we empty it. *Length* is a word used to describe a wine that gives an impression of going all the way on the palate — you can taste it across the full length of your tongue — instead of stopping short halfway through your tasting of it. Many wines today are very upfront on the palate — they make a big impression as soon as you taste them — but they don't go the distance in your mouth; they're *short.* Generally, high alcohol or excess tannin is to blame. Length is a sure sign of high quality.

✔ **Depth:** This is another subjective, unmeasurable attribute of a high-quality wine. We say a wine has *depth* when it seems to have a dimension of verticality — that is, it does not taste flat and one-dimensional in your mouth. A "flat" wine can never be great.

✔ **Complexity:** There's nothing wrong with a simple, straightforward wine, especially if you enjoy it. But a wine that keeps revealing different things about itself, always showing you a new flavor or impression — a wine that has *complexity* — is usually considered better quality. Some experts use the term *complexity* specifically to indicate that a wine has a multiplicity of aromas and flavors, while others use it in a more holistic (but less precise) sense, to refer to the total impression a wine gives you.

✔ **Finish:** The impression a wine leaves in the back of your mouth and in your throat after you've swallowed it is its *finish* or *aftertaste*. In a good wine, you can still perceive the wine's flavors — such as fruitiness or spiciness — at that point. Some wines may finish *hot,* because of high alcohol, or *bitter,* because of tannin — both shortcomings. Or a wine may have nothing much at all to say for itself after you swallow.

✔ **Typicity:** In order to judge whether a wine is true to its type, you have to know how that type is supposed to taste. So you have to know the textbook characteristics of wines made from the major grape varieties and wines of the world's classic wine regions. (For example, the Cabernet

Sauvignon grape typically has an aroma and flavor of black currants, and the French white wine called Pouilly-Fumé typically has a slight gunflint aroma.) Turn to Chapter 3 for those details.

What's a bad wine?

 Strangely enough, the right to declare a wine "good" because you like it does not carry with it the right to call a wine "bad" just because you don't. In this game, you get to make your own rules, but you don't get to force other people to live by them.

The fact is there are very few bad wines in the world today compared to even 20 years ago. And many of the wines we could call bad are actually just bad *bottles* of wine — bottles that were handled badly, so that the good wine inside them got ruined.

Here are some characteristics that everyone agrees indicate a bad wine. We hope you never meet one.

- ✔ **Moldy fruit:** Have you ever eaten a raspberry from the bottom of the container that had a dusty, cardboardy taste to it? That same taste of rot can be in a wine if the wine was made from grapes that were not completely fresh and healthy when they were harvested. Bad wine.

- ✔ **Vinegar:** In the natural evolution of things, wine is just a passing stage between grape juice and vinegar. Most wines today remain forever in the wine stage because of technology or careful winemaking. If you find a wine that has crossed the line toward vinegar, it's bad wine.

✔ **Chemical or bacterial smells:** The most common are acetone (nail-polish thinner) and sulfur flaws (rotten eggs, burnt rubber, bad garlic). Bad wines.

✔ **Oxidized wine:** This wine smells flat, weak, or maybe cooked, and it tastes the same. It may have been a good wine once, but air — oxygen — got in somehow and killed the wine. Bad bottle.

✔ **Cooked aromas and taste:** When a wine has been stored or shipped in heat, it can actually taste cooked or baked as a result. Often there's telltale leakage from the cork, or the cork has pushed up a bit. Bad bottle.

✔ **Corky wine:** The most common flaw, *corkiness* comes across as a smell of damp cardboard that gets worse with air, and a diminished flavor intensity. It's caused by a bad cork, and any wine in a bottle that's sealed with a cork is at risk for it. Bad bottle.

Chapter 3

Pinot Envy and Other Secrets about Grape Varieties

• •

In This Chapter

▶ Focusing on major grape varieties and their wines

▶ Defining *genus, species, variety, clone,* and other grape terms

▶ Looking at endangered species and mixed marriages

• •

*W*e love to visit wine country. Gazing across manicured rows of grapevines in Napa Valley or pondering craggy terraces of rugged hillside vines in Portugal inspires us — and reinforces for us the fact that wine is an agricultural product, born of the earth, the grapevine, and the hard work of humans. Literally and emotionally, grapes are the link between the land and the wine.

Grapes also happen to give us one of the easiest ways of classifying wine and making sense of the hundreds of different types of wine that exist.

Why Grapes Matter

Grapes are the starting point of every wine and, there-fore, they're largely responsible for the style and per-sonality of each wine. The grapes that make a particular wine dictate the genetic structure of that wine and how it will respond to everything that the winemaker does to it.

The specific grape variety (or varieties) that makes any given wine is largely responsible for the sensory characteristics the wine offers — from its appearance to its aromas, its flavors, and its alcohol–tannin–acid profile. How the grapes grow — the amount of sunshine and moisture they get, for example, and how ripe they are when they're harvested — can empha-size certain of their characteristics rather than others. So can winemaking processes such as oak aging.

Of genus and species

By *grape variety,* we mean the fruit of a specific type of grapevine: the fruit of the Cabernet Sauvignon vine, for example, or of the Chardonnay vine.

A variety of varieties

Snowflakes and fingerprints aren't the only examples of Nature's infinite variety. Within the genus *Vitis* and the species *vinifera,* there are as many as 10,000 varieties of wine grapes. Within those 10,000 varieties are grapes that have the ability to make extraordinary wine, grapes that tend to make very ordinary wine, and grapes that only a parent could love.

How grapes vary

All sorts of attributes distinguish each grape variety
from the next. These attributes fall into two categories:
personality traits and performance factors.

Personality traits of grape varieties

 Skin color is the most fundamental distinction
among grape varieties. Every grape variety
is considered either a white variety or a red
(or "black") one, according to the color of its
skins when the grapes are ripe. (A few red-
skinned varieties are further distinguished by
having red pulp rather than white pulp.)

Individual grape varieties also differ from one another
in other ways:

- **Aromatic compounds:** Some grapes (like Muscat)
contribute floral aromas and flavors to their wine,
for example, while other grapes contribute herbaceous notes (as Sauvignon Blanc does) or fruity
character. Some grapes have very neutral aromas
and flavors and, therefore, make fairly neutral
wines.

- **Acidity levels:** Some grapes are naturally disposed to higher acid levels than others, which
influences the wine made from those grapes.

- **Thickness of skin and size of the individual
grapes:** Black grapes with thick skins naturally
have more tannin than grapes with thin skins;
ditto for small-berried varieties compared to
large-berried varieties, because their skin-to-juice
ratio is higher. More tannin in the grapes translates into a firmer, more tannic red wine.

Performance factors of grape varieties

The performance factors that distinguish grape varieties are vitally important to the grape grower because those factors determine how easy or challenging it will be for him to cultivate a specific variety in his vineyard — if he can even grow it at all. The issues include

- ✔ **How much time a variety typically needs to ripen its grapes:** In regions with short growing seasons, early-ripening varieties do best.

- ✔ **How dense and compact the bunches of grapes are:** In warm, damp climates, grape varieties with dense bunches can have mildew problems.

- ✔ **How much vegetation a particular variety tends to grow:** In fertile soils, a vine that's disposed to growing a lot of leaves and shoots can have so much vegetation that the grapes don't get enough sun to ripen.

A Primer on White Grape Varieties

This section includes descriptions of the most important white *vinifera* varieties today. In describing the grapes, naturally we describe the types of wine that are made from each grape. These wines can be varietal wines, or place-name wines that don't mention the grape variety anywhere on the label (a common practice for European wines). These grapes can also be blending partners for other grapes, in wines made from multiple grape varieties.

Chardonnay

Chardonnay is a regal grape for its role in producing the greatest dry white wines in the world — white Burgundies — and for being one of the main grapes of Champagne. Today it also ends up in a huge amount of everyday wine.

The Chardonnay grape grows in practically every wine-producing country of the world, for two reasons: It's relatively adaptable to a wide range of climates; and the name Chardonnay on a wine label is, these days, a surefire sales tool.

Because the flavors of Chardonnay are very compatible with those of oak — and because white Burgundy (the great prototype) is generally an oaked wine, and because many wine drinkers love the flavor of oak — most Chardonnay wine receives some oak treatment either during or after fermentation. (For the best Chardonnays, oak treatment means expensive barrels of French oak; but for lower-priced Chardonnays it could mean soaking oak chips in the wine or even adding liquid essence of oak.) Except for Northeastern Italy and France's Chablis and Mâconnais districts, where oak is usually not used for Chardonnay, oaky Chardonnay wine is the norm and unoaked Chardonnay is the exception.

Chardonnay itself has fruity aromas and flavors that range from apple — in cooler wine regions — to tropical fruits, especially pineapple, in warmer regions. Chardonnay also can display subtle earthy aromas, such as mushroom or minerals. Chardonnay wine has medium to high acidity and is generally full-bodied. Classically, Chardonnay wines are dry. But most inexpensive Chardonnays these days are actually a bit sweet.

Chardonnay is a grape that can stand on its own in a wine, and the top Chardonnay-based wines (except for Champagne and similar bubblies) are 100 percent Chardonnay. But less-expensive wines that are labeled *Chardonnay* — those selling for less than $10 a bottle in the United States, for example — are likely to have some other, far less distinguished grape blended in, to help reduce the cost of making the wine. Anyway, who can even tell, behind all that oak?

Riesling

The great Riesling wines of Germany have put the Riesling grape on the charts as an undisputedly noble variety. Riesling shows its real class only in a few places outside of Germany, however. The Alsace region of France, Austria, and the Clare Valley region of Australia are among the few.

Riesling wines are far less popular today than Chardonnay. Maybe that's because Riesling is the antithesis of Chardonnay. While Chardonnay is usually gussied up with oak, Riesling almost never is; while Chardonnay can be full-bodied and rich, Riesling is more often light-bodied, crisp, and refreshing. Riesling's fresh, vivid personality can make many Chardonnays taste clumsy in comparison.

The common perception of Riesling wines is that they're sweet, and many of them are — but plenty of them aren't. Alsace Rieslings are normally dry, many German Rieslings are fairly dry, and a few American Rieslings are dry. (Riesling can be vinified either way, according to the style of wine a producer wants to make.) Look for the word *trocken* (meaning dry) on

German Riesling labels and the word *dry* on
American labels if you prefer the dry style of
Riesling.

High acidity, low to medium alcohol levels, and
aromas/flavors that range from ebulliently fruity to
flowery to minerally are trademarks of Riesling.

Riesling wines are sometimes labeled as
White Riesling or *Johannisberg Riesling* — both
synonyms for the noble Riesling grape. With
wines from Eastern European countries,
though, read the fine print: Olazrizling,
Laskirizling, and Welschriesling are from
another grape altogether.

Sauvignon Blanc

Sauvignon Blanc is a white variety with a very distinc-
tive character. It's high in acidity with pronounced
aromas and flavors. Besides herbaceous character
(sometimes referred to as *grassy*), Sauvignon Blanc
wines display mineral aromas and flavors, vegetal character, or — in certain climates — fruity character, such
as ripe melon, figs, or passion fruit. The wines are light-
to medium-bodied and usually dry. Most of them are
unoaked, but some are oaky.

France has two classic wine regions for the Sauvignon
Blanc grape: Bordeaux; and the Loire Valley, where the
two best known Sauvignon wines are called Sancerre or
Pouilly-Fumé. In Bordeaux, Sauvignon Blanc is sometimes blended with Sémillon; some of the wines that
are blended about 50-50 from the two grapes and fermented in oak are among the great white wines of the
world.

Sauvignon Blanc is also important in northeastern Italy, South Africa, and parts of California, where the wines are sometimes labeled as "Fumé Blanc." New Zealand's Sauvignon Blanc wines in particular are renowned for their fresh, flavorful style.

Pinot Gris/Pinot Grigio

Pinot Gris *(gree)* is one of several grape varieties called *Pinot:* Pinot Blanc (white Pinot), Pinot Noir (black Pinot), Pinot Meunier (we don't know how that one translates), and Pinot Gris (gray Pinot), which is called *Pinot Grigio* in Italian. Pinot Gris is believed to have mutated from the black Pinot Noir grape. Although it's considered a white grape, its skin color is unusually dark for a white variety.

Wines made from Pinot Gris can be deeper in color than most white wines — although most of Italy's Pinot Grigio wines are quite pale. Pinot Gris wines are medium- to full-bodied, usually not oaky, and have rather low acidity and fairly neutral aromas. Sometimes the flavor and aroma can suggest the skins of fruit, such as peach skins or orange rind.

Pinot Gris is an important grape throughout northeastern Italy, and it also grows in Germany, where it is called Ruländer. The only region in France where Pinot Gris is important is in Alsace, where it really struts its stuff. Oregon has had good success with Pinot Gris, and more and more winemakers in California are now taking a shot at it. Because Pinot Grigio is one of the best-selling inexpensive white wines in the United States, countries such as Chile and Australia now grow this grape for mass-market wines, and they often call the wine "Pinot Grigio."

A Primer on Red Grape Varieties

Here are descriptions of important red *vinifera* grape varieties. You'll encounter these grapes in varietal wines and also in place-name wines.

Cabernet Sauvignon

Cabernet Sauvignon is a noble grape variety that grows well in just about any climate that isn't very cool. It became famous through the age-worthy red wines of the Médoc district of Bordeaux (which usually also contain Merlot and Cabernet Franc, in varying proportions). But today California is an equally important region for Cabernet Sauvignon — not to mention Washington, southern France, Italy, Australia, South Africa, Chile, Argentina, and so on.

The Cabernet Sauvignon grape makes wines that are high in tannin and are medium- to full-bodied. The text-book descriptor for Cabernet Sauvignon's aroma and flavor is *black currants* or *cassis;* the grape can also contribute vegetal tones to a wine when or where the grapes are less than ideally ripe.

 Cabernet Sauvignon wines come in all price and quality levels. The least-expensive versions are usually fairly soft and very fruity, with medium body. The best wines are rich and firm with great depth and classic Cabernet flavor. Serious Cabernet Sauvignons can age for 15 years or more.

Because Cabernet Sauvignon is fairly tannic (and because of the blending precedent in Bordeaux), winemakers often blend it with other grapes; usually Merlot — being less tannic — is considered an ideal

partner. Australian winemakers have an unusual practice of blending Cabernet Sauvignon with Syrah.

Merlot

Deep color, full body, high alcohol, and low tannin are
the characteristics of wines made from the Merlot
grape. The aromas and flavors can be plummy or sometimes chocolatey, or they can suggest tea leaves.

 Some wine drinkers find Merlot easier to like
than Cabernet Sauvignon because it's less
tannic. (But some winemakers feel that Merlot
isn't satisfactory in its own right and, thus,
often blend it with Cabernet Sauvignon,
Cabernet Franc, or both.) Merlot makes both
inexpensive, simple wines and, when grown in
the right conditions, very serious wines.

Merlot is actually the most-planted grape variety in
Bordeaux, where it excels in the Right Bank districts
of Pomerol and St. Emilion. Merlot is also important
in Washington, California, the Long Island district of
New York, northeastern Italy, and Chile.

Pinot Noir

Pinot Noir is finicky, troublesome, enigmatic, and
challenging. But a great Pinot Noir can be one of the
greatest wines ever.

The prototype for Pinot Noir wine is red Burgundy,
from France, where tiny vineyard plots yield rare trea-
sures of wine made entirely from Pinot Noir. Oregon,
California, New Zealand, and parts of Australia and
Chile also produce good Pinot Noir. But Pinot Noir's
production is rather limited, because this variety is
very particular about climate and soil.

Pinot Noir wine is lighter in color than Cabernet or Merlot. It has relatively high alcohol, medium to high acidity, and medium to low tannin (although oak barrels can contribute additional tannin to the wine). Its flavors and aromas can be very fruity — often like a mélange of red berries — or earthy and woodsy, depending on how it is grown and/or vinified. Pinot Noir is rarely blended with other grapes.

Syrah/Shiraz

The northern part of France's Rhône Valley is the classic home for great wines from the Syrah grape. Rhône wines such as Hermitage and Côte-Rôtie are the inspiration for Syrah's dissemination to Australia, California, Washington, Italy, and Spain.

Syrah produces deeply colored wines with full body, firm tannin, and aromas/flavors that can suggest berries, smoked meat, black pepper, tar, or even burnt rubber (believe it or not). In Australia, Syrah (called Shiraz) comes in several styles — some of them charming, medium-bodied, vibrantly fruity wines that are quite the opposite of the Northern Rhône's powerful Syrahs.

Syrah doesn't require any other grape to complement its flavors, although in Australia it is often blended with Cabernet, and in the Southern Rhône it is often part of a blended wine with Grenache and other varieties.

Zinfandel

White Zinfandel is such a popular wine — and so much better known than the red style of Zinfandel — that its fans might argue that Zinfandel is a white grape. But it's really red.

Zin — as lovers of red Zinfandel call it — makes rich, dark wines that are high in alcohol and medium to high in tannin. They can have a blackberry or raspberry aroma and flavor, a spicy or tarry character, or even a jammy flavor. Some Zins are lighter than others and meant to be enjoyed young, and some are serious wines with a tannin structure that's built for aging. (You can tell which is which by the price.)

Nebbiolo

Outside of scattered sites in northwestern Italy — mainly the Piedmont region — Nebbiolo just doesn't make remarkable wine. But the extraordinary quality of Barolo and Barbaresco, two Piedmont wines, prove what greatness it can achieve under the right conditions.

The Nebbiolo grape is high in both tannin and acid, which can make a wine tough. Fortunately, it also gives enough alcohol to soften the package. Its color can be deep when the wine is young but can develop orangey tinges within a few years. Its complex aroma is fruity (strawberry, cherry), earthy and woodsy (tar, truffles), herbal (mint, eucalyptus, anise), and floral (roses).

Lighter versions of Nebbiolo are meant to be drunk young — wines labeled Nebbiolo d'Alba, Roero, or Nebbiolo delle Langhe, for example — while Barolo and Barbaresco are wines that really deserve a *minimum* of eight years of age before drinking.

Sangiovese

This Italian grape has proven itself in the Tuscany region of Italy, especially in the Brunello di Montalcino and Chianti districts. Sangiovese makes wines that are medium to high in acidity and firm in tannin; the wines can be light-bodied to full-bodied, depending on exactly where the grapes grow and how the wine is made. The aromas and flavors of the wines are fruity — especially cherry, often tart cherry — with floral nuances of violets and sometimes a slightly nutty character.

Tempranillo

Tempranillo is Spain's candidate for greatness. It gives wines deep color, low acidity, and only moderate alcohol. Modern renditions of Tempranillo from the Ribera del Duero region and elsewhere in Spain prove what color and fruitiness this grape has. In more traditional wines, such as those of the Rioja region, much of the grape's color and flavor is lost due to long wood aging and to blending with varieties that lack color, such as Grenache.

Chapter 4

The Insider's Track to Serving and Using Wine

. . . .

In This Chapter

▶ Overcoming corkophobia and other barriers to getting the wine out

▶ Serving wine at the right temperature

. . . .

*H*ave you ever broken a cork while trying to extract it from the bottle, or taken an unusually long time to remove a stubborn cork, while your guests smiled at you uneasily? This has certainly happened to us from time to time and probably to just about everyone else who has ever pulled a cork out of a bottle of wine. It's enough to give anyone a case of corkophobia!

Removing the cork from a wine bottle is the first challenge you face in your quest to enjoy wine, and it's a big one. (Fortunately, once you get the hang of it, it's easy — most of the time.) Afterwards, there are the niggling details of wine service, such as what temperature to serve the wine. But help is at hand for the wine-challenged!

Getting the Cork Out

Before you can even think about removing the cork from a wine bottle, you need to deal with whatever covers the cork. Most wine bottles have a colorful covering over the top of the bottle that's called a *capsule.* Wineries place capsules on top of the corks for two reasons: to keep the corks clean, and to create a fetching look for their bottles.

Whether the capsule is plastic, foil, or cellophane, remove the entire capsule, so that no wine can possibly come into contact with the covering when you pour. (Use the small knife that's part of most *corkscrews* — the devices that exist solely for opening wine bottles.) When you encounter a plastic plug atop the cork instead of a capsule, just flick it off with the tip of a knife.

After removing the capsule or plug, wipe clean the top of the bottle with a damp cloth. Sometimes the visible end of the cork is dark with mold that developed under the capsule; in that case, wipe all the more diligently. (If you encounter mold atop the cork, don't be concerned. That mold is actually a good sign: It means that the wine has been stored in humid conditions.)

Sometimes wine lovers just can't bring themselves to remove the whole capsule out of respect for the bottle of wine that they're about to drink. (In fact, traditional wine etiquette dictates that you not remove the entire capsule.) Many people use a gizmo called a *foil cutter* that sells for about $7 in wine shops, kitchen stores, or specialty catalogs. However, the foil cutter doesn't cut the capsule low enough, in our opinion, to prevent wine from dripping over the edge of the foil into the glass. If you want to leave the capsule on, use the corkscrew's knife to cut the foil under the second lip of the bottle, approximately ¾ inch from the top.

The corkscrew not to use

The one corkscrew we absolutely avoid happens to be the most common type of corkscrew around. We don't like it for one very simple reason: It mangles the cork, almost guaranteeing that brown flakes will be floating in your glass of wine.

That corkscrew is the infamous wing-type corkscrew, a bright silver-colored, metal device that looks like a cross between a pair of pliers and a drill; when you insert this corkscrew into a cork, two "wings" open out from the side of the corkscrew. The major shortcoming of this device is its very short worm, or *auger* (the curly prong that bores into the cork), which is too short for many corks and overly aggressive on all of them.

Invest a few dollars in a decent corkscrew right off the bat. The time and hassle you'll save will be more than worth the investment. Of the many types of wine-bottle openers available, we recommend the three described in the following sections.

The corkscrew to buy

The one indispensable corkscrew for every household is the Screwpull. It was invented in the early 1980s by a renowned Houston scientist, Dr. Herbert Allen, who was apparently tired of having a 10¢ piece of cork get the better of him.

The Screwpull is about 6 inches long. It consists of an arched piece of plastic (which looks like a clothespin on steroids) straddling an inordinately long, 5-inch worm that's coated with Teflon (see Figure 4-1).

To use this corkscrew, you simply place the plastic over the bottle top (having already removed the capsule), until a lip on the plastic is resting on the top of the bottle. Insert the worm through the plastic, until it touches the cork. Hold on to the plastic firmly while turning the lever atop the worm clockwise. The worm descends into the cork. Then you simply keep turning the lever in the same clockwise direction, and the cork magically emerges from the bottle. To remove the cork from the Screwpull, simply turn the lever counterclockwise while holding on to the cork.

The Screwpull comes in many colors and costs about $20 in wine shops, kitchen stores, and specialty catalogs. It's very simple to use, doesn't require a lot of muscle, and is our corkscrew of choice for most of the corks that we encounter.

© *Akira Chiwaki*

Figure 4-1: The Screwpull corkscrew.

The Screwpull has one drawback; because it's made of plastic, it can break. But now a stainless steel version is available, for about $30. This Screwpull should last indefinitely.

Other corkscrews worth owning

Although we favor the Screwpull for removing corks, we have two other corkscrews for the remaining corks that the Screwpull can't remove.

The two-pronged type that they use in California

One is called, unofficially, the Ah-So because (according to wine legend, anyway) when people finally figure out how it works, they say, "Ah, so that's how it works!" (It's also known as the "Butler's Friend" — but where have all the butlers gone?)

It's a simple device made up of two thin, flat, metal prongs, one slightly longer than the other (see Figure 4-2). To use it, you slide the prongs down into the tight space between the cork and the bottle (inserting the longer prong first), using a back-and-forth seesaw motion until the top of the Ah-So is resting on the top of the cork. Then you twist the cork while gently pulling it up.

One advantage of the Ah-So is that it delivers an intact cork — without a hole in it — that can be reused to close bottles of homemade vinegar, or to make cutesy bulletin boards.

Although more difficult to operate than the Screwpull, the Ah-So really comes into its own with very tight-fitting corks that no other corkscrews, including the Screwpull, seem to be able to budge. Also, the Ah-So can be effective with old, crumbly corks that don't give other corkscrews much to grip.

© Akira Chiwaki

Figure 4-2: The Ah-So corkscrew.

The Ah-So is useless with loose corks that move around in the bottle's neck when you try to remove them. It just pushes those corks down into the wine. At that point, you'll need another tool called a *cork retriever* (which we describe in the "Waiter, there's cork in my wine!" sidebar, in this chapter).

The Ah-So sells for around $6 to $9. It seems to be especially popular in California for no particular reason that we've ever been able to figure out.

The most professional corkscrew of them all

Our final recommended corkscrew, probably the most commonly used corkscrew in restaurants all over the world, is simply called the waiter's corkscrew. A straight or gently curved base holds three devices that fold into it, like a Swiss Army knife: a lever, a worm, and a small knife (see Figure 4-3). The latter is especially handy for removing the capsule from the bottle.

© *Akira Chiwaki*

Figure 4-3: The waiter's corkscrew.

Using the waiter's corkscrew requires some practice. First, wrap your fist around the bottle's neck. The trick then is to guide the worm down through the center of the cork, by turning the corkscrew; turn slowly at first, until you're sure that the worm is not off center and actually is descending down the middle of the cork. After the worm is fully descended into the cork, place the lever on the lip of the bottle and push against the lever while pulling the cork up. Give a firm tug at the very end or wiggle the bottom of the cork out with your hand.

Waiter, there's cork in my wine!

Every now and then, even if you've used the right corkscrew and used it properly, you can still have pieces of cork floating in your wine. They can be tiny dry flakes that crumbled into the bottle, actual chunks of cork, or even the entire cork.

Before you start berating yourself for being a klutz, you should know that "floating cork" has happened to all of us at one time or another, no matter how experienced we are. Cork won't harm the wine. And besides, there's a wonderful instrument called a *cork retriever* available in specialty stores and in catalogs (although it's considerably more difficult to find than a corkscrew).

The cork retriever consists of three 10-inch pieces of stiff metal wire with hooks on the ends. This device is remarkably effective for removing floating pieces of cork from the bottle. We've even removed a whole cork from the neck with a cork retriever (fearing the whole time that the bottle neck would explode when we tried to force the cork *and* the retriever back up through the tiny diameter).

Your other option is to just pick out the offending piece(s) of cork with a spoon after you pour the wine into your glass. (That's one occasion when it's rude to serve your guest first, because the first glass has more cork pieces in it.) Or you can pour the wine through a paper coffee filter (preferably the natural brown-paper filter, or a filter rinsed with hot water to remove the chemicals) into a decanter or pitcher to catch the remaining pieces of cork.

If your cork ever breaks and part of it gets stuck in the neck of the bottle, the waiter's corkscrew is indispensable for removing the remaining piece. Use the method we just described, but insert the worm at a 45-degree angle. In most cases, you'll successfully remove the broken cork.

The waiter's corkscrew sells for as little as $7, but designer versions can cost more than ten times that much.

A special case: Opening Champagne and sparkling wine

Opening a bottle of sparkling wine is usually an exciting occasion. Who doesn't enjoy the ceremony of a cold glass of bubbly? But you need to use a completely different technique than you'd use to open a regular wine bottle. The cork even looks different. Sparkling wine corks have a mushroom-shape head that protrudes from the bottle and a wire cage that holds the cork in place against the pressure that's trapped inside the bottle.

 Never, ever use a corkscrew on a bottle of sparkling wine. The pressure of the trapped carbonation, when suddenly released, can send the cork *and* corkscrew flying right into your eye.

Forget how they do it in locker rooms

 If your bottle of bubbly has just traveled, let it rest for a while, preferably a day. Controlling the cork is difficult when the carbonation has been stirred up. (Hey, you wouldn't open a large bottle of soda that's warm and shaken up, either, would you? Sparkling wine has much more carbonated pressure than soda, and it needs more time to settle down.)

If you're in the midst of a sparkling-wine emergency and need to open the bottle anyway, one quick solution is to calm down the carbonation by submerging the bottle in an ice bucket for about 30 minutes. (Fill the bucket with one-half ice cubes and one-half ice-cold water.)

In any case, be careful when you remove the wire cage, and keep one hand on top of the cork as a precaution. (We had a hole in our kitchen ceiling from one adventure with a flying cork.) Be sure to point the bottle away from people and other fragile objects.

A sigh is better than a pop

If you like to hear the cork pop, just yank it out. When you do that, however, you'll lose some of the precious wine, which will froth out of the bottle. Also, the noise can interfere with your guests' conversation. Besides, it ain't too classy!

Removing the cork from sparkling wine with just a gentle sigh rather than a loud pop is fairly easy. Simply hold the bottle at a 45-degree angle with a towel wrapped around it if it's wet. (Try resting the base of the bottle on your hipbone.) Twist the bottle while holding onto the cork so that you can control the cork as it emerges. When you feel the cork starting to come out of the bottle, *push down against the cork* with some pressure, as if you don't want to let it out of the bottle. In this way, the cork will emerge slowly with a hiss or sigh sound rather than a pop.

 Every once in a while, you'll come across a really tight sparkling-wine cork that doesn't want to budge. Try running the top of the bottle under warm water for a few minutes, or wrapping a towel around the cork to create friction. Either action will usually enable you to remove the cork.

Another option is to purchase a fancy gadget that you place around the part of the cork that's outside the bottle. (There are actually three gadgets: Champagne pliers, a Champagne star, and a Champagne key.) Or you could probably try using regular pliers, although lugging in the toolbox will surely change the mood of the occasion.

Not Too Warm, Not Too Cold

Serving wine at the ideal temperature is a vital factor in your enjoyment of wine. Frequently, we've tasted the same wine at different temperatures and have loved the wine on one occasion but disliked it the other!

Just as many red wines are served too warm, most white wines are definitely served too cold, judging by the service that we've received in many restaurants. The higher the quality of a white wine, the less cold it should be, so that you can properly appreciate its flavor.

Here are our recommended serving temperatures for various types of wines:

- ✔ **Most Champagnes and sparkling wines:** 45°F
- ✔ **Older or expensive, complex Champagnes:** 52°F–54°F
- ✔ **Inexpensive sweet wines:** 50°F–55°F
- ✔ **Rosés and blush wines:** 50°F–55°F
- ✔ **Simpler, inexpensive, quaffing-type white wines:** 50°F–55°F
- ✔ **Dry Sherry, such as fino or manzanilla:** 55°F–56°F
- ✔ **Fine, dry white wines:** 58°F–62°F
- ✔ **Finer dessert wines, such as a good Sauternes:** 58°F–62°F
- ✔ **Light, fruity red wines:** 58°F–60°F
- ✔ **Most red wines:** 62°F–65°F
- ✔ **Sherry other than dry fino or manzanilla:** 62°F–65°F
- ✔ **Port:** 62°F–65°F

Are you wondering how to know when your bottle is the right temperature? You can buy a nifty digital thermometer that wraps around the outside of the bottle and gives you a color-coded reading. Or you can buy something that looks like a real thermometer that you place into the opened bottle (in the bottle's mouth, you might say). We have both of those, and we never use them. Just feel the bottle with your hand and take a guess. Practice makes perfect.

Half-empty or half-full?

"Fill 'er up" may be the rule for your gas tank, but not for your wine glass. We're annoyed when servers fill our glasses to the top. We guess they don't want to bother repouring the wine too often. Or maybe they want to give us our money's worth. But how can we stick our noses into full glasses without looking like idiots?

To leave some margin of safety for swirling and smelling the wine, fill the glass only partially. One-third capacity is the best fill level for serious red wines. (This goes back to that idea of aerating the wine.) White-wine glasses can be filled halfway, while sparkling-wine glasses can be three-quarters full.

Want more?

Visit **www.dummies.com/go/target** to get related articles, videos, or illustrated step-by-steps on your favorite Dummies title.

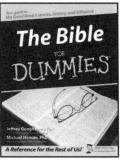

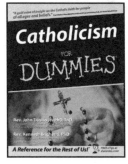

Making Everything Easier!™

6th Edition

Personal Finance

FOR DUMMIES

Learn to:
- Assess your financial fitness
- Save more and spend less
- Review your credit report and improve your score
- Make smart investments in any economic environment

Eric Tyson, MBA
Bestselling author of Investing For Dummies

Now updated! The bestselling guide to managing your diabetes
featuring coverage of the latest treatments

Diabetes

FOR DUMMIES

3rd Edition

Alan L. Rubin, MD

A Reference for the Rest of Us!

Covers the iPhone, iPhone 3G, and iPhone 3G S!

3rd Edition

iPhone

FOR DUMMIES

Learn to:
- Set up your iPhone, send and receive e-mail, and browse the Internet
- Shoot great videos and take and share photos
- Use GPS maps, listen to music, and download your favorite apps

IN FULL COLOR!

Edward C. Baig
Bob "Dr. Mac" LeVitus

Making Everything Easier!™

4th Edition

iPod & iTunes

FOR DUMMIES

Learn to:
- Set up iTunes and your iPod
- Shop at the iTunes Store
- Manage photos and videos on your iPod
- Add music tracks from a CD to your iTunes library

Tony Bove

Want more?

Visit **www.dummies.com/go/target** to get related articles, videos, or illustrated step-by-steps on your favorite Dummies title.

With more than 1,600 titles to choose from, we've got a Dummies Book for wherever you are in life! Look for Dummies titles wherever books are sold, call 877-762-2974, or visit *dummies.com*.